MY HEART IS LIKE A Singing BIRD

INSPIRING QUOTES TO COLOR AND KEEP

hinkler

THE
FAMILY
IS ONE OF
Nature's
MASTERPIECES
— GEORGE SANTAYANA —

HOPE

is the only bee that makes honey without flowers.

Robert Green Ingersoll

The only limitations are the ones we put on ourselves.

Ita Buttrose

The way to get started
is to quit talking
and begin doing.

Walt Disney

Storms make trees
take deeper roots.

Dolly Parton

The best and most beautiful things in life cannot be seen, nor touched, but are felt in the heart.

Helen Keller

Life shrinks or expands in
proportion to one's courage.

Anais Nin

For a caterpillar to become a butterfly, it must change.

Unknown

HAPPINESS is a PERFUME you cannot pour on Others without getting a few drops on YOURSELF

Ralph Waldo Emerson

You must recognize

the value of the moment.

Halina Wagowska

A good head and a good heart

are always a formidable combination.

Nelson Mandela

You simply have to put one foot in front of the other and keep going.

George Lucas

Far away in the sunshine are my highest aspirations.
I may not reach them, but I can look up and see their beauty,
believe in them, and try to follow where they lead.

Louisa May Alcott

No bird soars too high if he
soars with his own wings.

William Blake

Life itself is the most wonderful fairy tale.

Hans Christian Andersen

→↓↓ ⇒⇒ ↑↗⇒↓↓←↓↓⇒↠

With the
new day
comes
new strength
and
new thoughts.

Eleanor Roosevelt

THERE IS NO *Love* SINCERER THAN THE *love* OF FOOD

GEORGE BERNARD SHAW

We have only this **moment**,
sparkling like a **star**
in our hand—and melting like
a **snowflake**...

Marie Beyon Ray

Beauty is not in the face;

beauty is a light in the heart.

Khalil Gibran

Earth laughs in flowers.

Ralph Waldo Emerson

WHEN TEA
BECOMES
RITUAL,
IT TAKES
ITS PLACE
AT THE
HEART
OF OUR
ABILITY
TO SEE
GREATNESS
IN
SMALL
THINGS.
MURIEL BARBERY

Love is a canvas, furnished by nature

and embroidered by the imagination.

Voltaire

Be happy. It's one way of being wise.

Sidonie Gabrielle Collete

Autumn is a second spring when
every leaf is a flower.
Albert Camus

I have always been
delighted at the prospect
of a new day, a fresh try,
one more start, with perhaps a
bit of magic waiting somewhere
behind the morning.

J. B. Priestley

Whenever you are
creating beauty
around you,
you are restoring
your own soul.

Alice Walker

Home is not where you live but where they understand you.

Christian Morgenstern

Passion is energy.
Feel the power that comes from
focusing on what excites you.

Oprah Winfrey

Nature uses human imagination to lift he of creation to even higher levels.

Luigi Pirandello

We do not see nature with our eyes, but with our understandings and our hearts.

William Hazlitt

Logic will get you from **A** *to* **B**.
Imagination will take you *everywhere*.

Albert Einstein

Just living is not enough...
one must have sunshine,
freedom, and a little flower.

Hans Christian Andersen

I now believe that pain makes you stronger, and now I believe that walking through a lot of rainstorms gets you clean.

Taylor Swift

We can never obtain peace in the outer world
until we obtain peace with ourselves.

Dalai Lama

Whatever we lose
(like a you or a me),
it's always ourselves we
find in the sea.

E. E. Cummings

There are always flowers for those who want to see them.

Henri Matisse

Hope is like the sun, which as we journey towards it, casts the shadow of our burdens behind us.

Samuel Smiles

Only those who will risk going too f[ar]
can possibly find out how far one can [go]

T. S. Eliot

DON'T JUDGE EACH day by the HARVEST You reap but by the SEEDS THAT YOU PLANT

ROBERT LOUIS STEVENSON

⌀ + ⌀ + ⋔

Sila